Family World

My Sister

Caryn Jenner

W
FRANKLIN WATTS
LONDON•SYDNEY

Sharing this book

This book shows the relationships of sisters with their siblings in children's lives around the world. It provides a useful starting point to discuss how families everywhere are similar, but that each child's family is different and special.

• Remember that families are formed in different ways and a sister can be a step-sister, half-sister, adoptive sister, foster sister or any girl that a child thinks of as a sister.
• Family life is rewarding, but sometimes it can also be difficult. Ask your GP, health visitor or school for advice. These organisations also offer help to families:

Family Lives – www.familylives.org.uk; Parentline 0808 800 2222
Family Links – www.familylinks.org.uk
Gingerbread (especially for single-parent families) – www.gingerbread.org.uk

Franklin Watts
Published in Great Britain in 2017
by The Watts Publishing Group

Copyright © The Watts Publishing Group, 2017

All rights reserved.

Series Editor: Sarah Peutrill
Series Designer: Ruth Walton

Dewey number: 306.8'742
ISBN: 978 1 4451 5240 0

Printed in Singapore

Franklin Watts
An imprint of Hachette Children's Group
Part of The Watts Publishing Group
Carmelite House, 50 Victoria Embankment
London EC4Y 0DZ

An Hachette UK Company
www.hachette.co.uk
www.franklinwatts.co.uk

Picture credits:
AISPIX/Shutterstock: 8, 22. Felix Alim/istockphoto: 15. BartCo/istockphoto: 11. Beboy Ltd/istockphoto: 23ccr. Mark Bowden/istockphoto: 23bl. Robert Churchill/istockphoto: back cover, 4. Distinctive Images/Shutterstock: 10b. drbimages/istockphoto: 23c.gabor2100/Shutterstock: 20-21. Rosemarie Gearhart/istockphoto: 23bc. Jenkedco/Shutterstock: 17b. Jacek Kadaj/Shutterstock: 6c. kali9/istockphoto: 23tcr. Paul Kline/istockphoto: 23br. Linda Kloosterhof/istockphoto: front cover, 7. Nolte Lourens/Shutterstock: 6b. Steve Luker/istockphoto: 23tl, 23tcl. Ian Machellan/Shutterstock: 18. meshaphoto//istockphoto: 23cr.Monkey Business/Shutterstock: 17t. Nicholas Monu/istockphoto: 23tr. Neustockimages/istockphoto: 23ccl. Robert Nystrom/istockphoto: 23cl. Saurabhpbhoyar/Shutterstock: 19. Mike Sonnenberg/istockphoto: 16.Stocklite/Shutterstock: 14b. Donatella Tandelli/Shutterstock: 5b. Vikran Raghu Vanshi/istockphoto: 5t. Claudia De Wald/istockphoto: 12. Piotr Wawrzynink/Shutterstock: 9t. Jaren Wicklund/istockphoto: 10c. Brad Wieland/istockphoto: 14t. Daman Yancy/Shutterstock: 9b. Zefei/Shutterstock: 13. Every attempt has been made to clear copyright. Should there be any inadvertent omission please apply to the publisher for rectification.

Please note: Some of the pictures in this book are posed by models. All scenarios are fictitious and any similarities to people, living or dead, are purely coincidental.

FSC
www.fsc.org
MIX
Paper from responsible sources
FSC® C104740

Contents

Sisters

Do you have a sister? Your sister is a girl with the same parents as you.

Enguun and her little sister,
Bayarma, live in Mongolia.
They play together every day.

There are four children in Sahila's family in India. As the oldest sister, Sahila tries to look after the younger ones.

In Australia, Shane's mum and step-dad have just had a baby called Hayley. She is Shane's half-sister.

How old?

You can have older sisters or younger sisters, or both! Twins or triplets are the same age.

Carlos and his sisters live in Peru. Alma is younger than Carlos, while Paloma is older. The children look after the family's alpacas.

Samuel's family lives in Uganda. His big sister, Femi, helps with his homework.

Yelena and Tatiana live in Russia. They are identical twin sisters so they look almost exactly alike.

?

Is your sister older or younger than you?

Sharing

You and your sister share lots of things. You share your family and home, as well as pets and toys.

Fortunata and Manuela like sharing a bedroom at their home in Venezuela. The sisters often giggle together at bedtime.

In Sweden, Becka's mum is married to Mia's dad, so the girls are step-sisters. They share their pet dog, Lars.

In Britain, Matilda and Alice take turns dipping their net into the pond. The girls are sisters because they were adopted into the same family.

? **What do you share with your sister?**

Getting along

When you get on well with your sister, you enjoy being together.

Jason and his step-sister, Kayla, live in the United States. They like going for a walk and talking about all sorts of things.

In Indonesia, Riya and her sister, Khadijah, play a clapping game together.

Jacintha and her sisters laugh as they swing on the hammock at their home in Suriname.

How do you feel when you and your sister are getting along well?

Everyone in a family can help each other.

Mosa is the youngest of four sisters who live in Uganda. In the mornings, all the sisters help each other get ready for school.

Jing Jing's family lives in China. When she sees that her sister, Lian, is sad, Jing Jing tries to make her feel better.

? **How do you and your sister help each other?**

Mucking about 😊

Sisters like to joke around and be silly – just like brothers do!

Estella and Rosario are sisters who live in Uruguay. They make each other laugh with their funny faces.

Kathleen and her half-sister, Bridget, like having pillow fights at their home in Ireland.

In Vietnam, Huy's little sister, An, likes kissing his cheek. Her kisses are so sloppy that Huy can't help laughing.

 **What makes you and your sister laugh?**

Getting cross

Sometimes sisters may make your cross! (Brothers too!)

Dylan's family is from Canada. When his sister, Abbie, puts grass down his back, Dylan tells her that he doesn't like it.

Ivan and his sister, Magda, live in Estonia. Sometimes they argue over the TV remote control and miss their favourite programmes.

In Guatemala, Felipe says he's very sorry that he made his sister Carlota angry.

?

How can you avoid arguing when you get cross?

Best friends

Sisters don't have to be just family. They can be best friends too!

Beatriz and Veronica like having parties together in El Salvador. They have lots of friends, but the two sisters are best friends forever.

Deepak's family lives in India. Deepak and his sister, Rani, know that they can always count on each other.

? How do you and your sister show that you're friends?

Canada

Great Britain

United States

Ireland

Guatemala

Venezuela

Suriname

A world of families

El Salvador

Peru

Children just like you live all around the world. Some children *have* sisters and some children *are* sisters. Every child's family is different and special in its own way, but families everywhere also have many things in common.

Uruguay

The families in this book live in the countries
marked on this map. Can you find the flag that
goes with each family in the book?

Activities

Make a star chart for you and your sister

See how well you can get along with your sister. Make a star chart to show how you are doing and give each other lots of stars for things like sharing and taking turns. Remember – if you make each other cross, then try to sort it out rather than arguing.

Find out how children around the world say 'sister'

Find out how to say sister in different languages. Ask friends who speak other languages, or look it up in books or on the Internet. Here are a few languages to get you started:

Russian – sestra

Spanish – hermana

French – sœur   Hindi – bahana

Chinese – jie jie (older sister); mei mei (younger sister)

Take turns choosing a game

First ask your sister what game she'd like to play. After you've played her game, then you choose a game to play. After a while, you'll make a habit of taking turns.

Make a family tree

A family tree shows the people in your family. Draw a picture of yourself and each person in your family, or use photos. On another sheet of paper, draw a tree. Stick your family pictures onto your tree. Your family tree can show the people you live with, or it can show lots of people in your family. You can even include your pets!

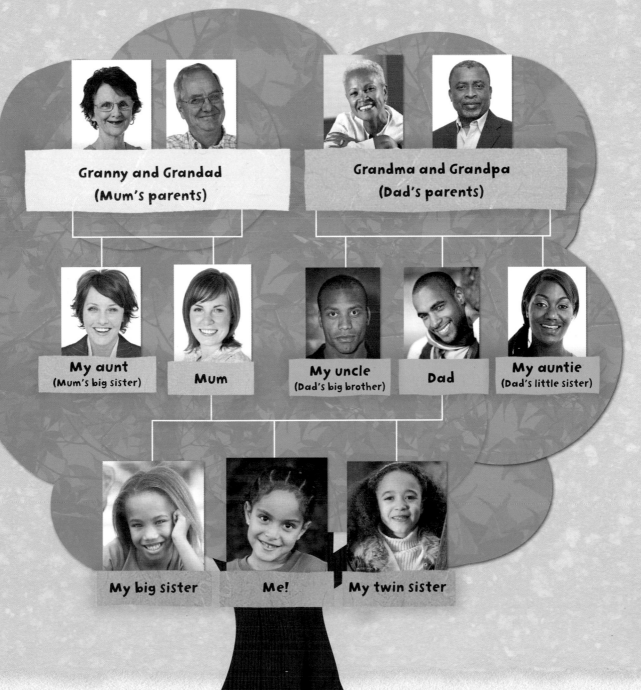

Granny and Grandad
(Mum's parents)

Grandma and Grandpa
(Dad's parents)

My aunt
(Mum's big sister)

Mum

My uncle
(Dad's big brother)

Dad

My auntie
(Dad's little sister)

My big sister

Me!

My twin sister

Words about families

Here are some words you may use when talking about families.

Adopted – becoming part of a family that is not the family you were born into

Divorced – when parents split up and are no longer married

Family – a group of people who love and care for each other and are usually related

Foster mum or dad – grown-ups who look after you in their family if your parents can't

Grandparents – your mum and dad's parents

Half-brother or half-sister – a brother or sister who has the same mum or dad as you, but the other parent is different

Parents – your mum and dad

Siblings – brothers and sisters

Step-brother or step-sister – the son or daughter of your step-mum or step-dad

Step-mum or step-dad – if your parents are divorced and one of them marries again, the new wife or husband would be your step-mum or step-dad

Index